MY FATHER MY SONS AND ME IN BETWEEN

RON TURNER

RADNOR PRESS

Nashville, Tennessee

My Father, My Sons and Me in Between

in memory of
my father,
Ennis Turner

. . . a good and
gentle man

CONTENTS

CONTENTS

CONTENTS

PREFACE

I'M A LAWYER. A few years ago I discovered I'm also a poet. It took a lot of courage to admit it. Lawyers are tough and brash, while poets are sensitive.

Since I started writing, I've met other lawyers (and nonlawyers alike) who quietly hide their creative sides.

If you're one of them, this book is for you; to encourage you to write, sketch, paint, photograph, sculpt, whittle, compose—whatever.

It doesn't matter whether you're any "good." The point is just do it. Be free. Create. You'll be more fun to be around and you'll be a better lawyer (or whatever) as well.

I suggest you read my stuff slowly, out loud. It may cause some strange looks from people sitting next to you at the airport. But what the heck, you're free, remember?

Go for it.

Ron Turner
August 3, 1997

TIME

TIME

I've always been fascinated by time. When we're children it won't move. Birthdays will never get here! Then around fifty they all begin to blur together.

Time is life. It is the ultimate gift to us. And our ultimate gift to others.

Guzzle Time

We
guzzle
time
like
soldiers
on
payday.

Thinking
it
will
never
end.

Grape Popsicles

Cold and
drippy on
muggy days
in the
Fifties
they were
my favorite.

Sitting
here all
grown up
eating one
feels funny.

Not
proper.
But just
right.

Ties

It was
one of
those calls
you don't
expect.

Dad
how do
you tie
a tie?

Knowing I
couldn't
do it over
the phone
I said
I'd be
right home.

Standing
eye to eye
with my
little boy
I see myself.

Wills

It's funny
how some
folks don't
have
a will.

They call
the lawyer
to talk
but never
get in
to sign.

Wills make
us face
who we love.
What we have.

Time.

Dog Shirts

They were
so cute
we all
stopped
and
watched.

Three
tow-headed
little
brothers
heading
up the
aisle of
the airport
shuttle.

Those are
great
shirts,
I said.

Remembering.

Stuff Of Life

With
precision
we measure
time.

Coming
going
going
coming

going
coming
coming
going.

Constant
backdrop
to
living.

Not
backdrop.

Life.

The Golden Ball

The boy and girl
squeal and
roll together
in the waves
fighting to keep
the golden ball.

Watch, Dad!
Daddy, watch!

He looks up
from his book
and freezes
the morning.

They laugh
as he runs
toward them.

Chasing the ball.

Old Pelican

He flies with old
but keen eyes.
Long beak.
Angular neck.

So many years soaring overhead
in cold and wind and rain.
Then swooping with ugly grace
to come up with food.
Or none.

He rests more often now.
To remember great fish.
To watch the young ones try.

For wisdom comes with time.
With more flights made
than to make.

Knowing that life
is not in coming back
with a full beak.

But in soaring high.
Swooping low.
And doing
it again.

Book Of Life

The boy steadies his glasses
and holds the big book
ready to read.

American Indians
and mountain men
and baseball and cats
fill the pages.

Soon the words get harder
and the reading slows
but he keeps on
as the story unfolds.

Characters appear
as well as plot.
Not knowing what's coming
he just can't stop.

Without warning one day he sees
more pages have been read
than there are to read.

The book's so good.
I want more, he cries.
But faster than ever
the words fly by.

Chapter.
Chapter.
Chapter.
Until one day.

It ends.

The Duet

In eighth
grade
a girl
asked me
to sing
a duet.

A lifetime
later I
hear it
and wonder
if I'm
forty-seven or
fourteen.

Or both.

Hurdles

It's the
closest
I ever came
to a blue
ribbon.

Running
hurdles
in
junior high
I looked
back.

Clear the
track,
the P.A.
cracked
as I
lay there.

Satchel
Page
was
right.

My MG

When I was 16
I saw it.
Hunter green
and tan inside.

MGBGT.
A mouthful of
letters I knew
I could never have.

A decade later
I saw it again.
Deep red this time
and I got it.

Now a generation
has passed and
it's a senior citizen.
I know it needs
the love of
an owner-mechanic.
But I'll miss it.

I'll miss
strangers'
looks.

I'll miss the
rumble even
when we're
not speeding.

I'll miss being 16.

Teeter-Totters

See-saw
margery
daw.

Remember
teeter
totters?

Now near
fifty the
challenge
remains.

Balance.

The Motorcycle

Eyes sparkling
a grin on his face
he straddles the seat
and slides into place.

Past fifty he rides
looking for more
than roads and streets
and trails to explore.

He has to touch
beyond his reach.
To ride and ride
his dreams to keep.

A boy again
he laughs without fear.
Fun again
after so many years.

Was It So Different?

My grandfathers
died before
I was born.

In their forties
in the Thirties
I wonder
what it was like.

With bills to pay.
Kids to raise.
Job stress.

Was it so different?

Go For It

I don't
want to be
looking up
at eighty
or ninety
wondering why
I didn't try.

MEN

MEN

I had never seen anything like it. On television one Sunday in 1990 Bill Moyers was interviewing a funny-talking man with white hair. The man was Robert Bly.

Bly talked about manhood; the difficulty of being a man in modern America. I sat transfixed, a long-quiet nerve touched.

That public television program and Bly's book, *Iron John,* led me to start writing poetry. I was overwhelmed with poems.

And I was amazed at how many of them dealt with my father, my sons and me in between.

Girls

I had a big brother
when I was little.
And two sons now.
Guess I'm an expert
on boys.

So why have I
wanted a girl?
I know they're
not always as
cute as they seem.

But there's something
about them
that balances the noise
and all the time
I've spent with boys.

Remembering

Just
as
the
man
was
in
the
boy
waiting

the
boy
is
in
the
man
remembering.

Sons Grow Up

Watching
my sons
grow up
doesn't make
me sad
the way
I thought
it would.

Manhood
hits
and
they're
themselves.

With a
little me
thrown in.

Sons and Daddies

It was easier
to be a son
than a daddy.

Daddies are
supposed
to be strong.

So where can
daddies go
when they hurt?

They want
to run to
their daddy
to find out
what to do
and there's
no daddy
to run to.

But them.

As I Play Father

It's the
best
advice
the old
man ever
gave me.

Take it
a day
at a
time.

Thirty
years
later
I hear
him as
I play
father.

Men Friends

One
is wise
and
witty.

One
thinks
deep.

One
hurts
as I
hurt.

Monthly
or less
over
lunch
or coffee
it's clear.

We share
dreams
no one else
hears.

The Men's Group

Something
happens
when we
close
the door.

Leaving
masks
outside
we laugh
and cry
and pray.

Unafraid.

Sawdust

He can't
explain
it.

Why hours
in his
shop
touch
his soul.

He can't
explain
it.

But he
was relieved
when she
agreed
that in
their
house
sawdust
is not
dirt.

Mr. Bacon

That's what
the boys
called him
years ago.

A Scoutmaster
before he
had sons
of his own
he loved it.

But work
and moves
and time
took him
away from
the woods.

Years
later with
men he
hardly
knows he
camps and
laughs.

Fixing
more
than bacon.

A Man One Day

Remember
when you were a boy
and dreamed
of being a man?

Of being tall
with
itchy whiskers.
Rumbly voice.

Magic smell
of tobacco.
Aftershave.

Now
you're
there.

It's all
you
dreamed.

And
less.

Lawyer's Lament

They were so proud.
You're going to law school!
Fine, they said.
They were so proud.

Before you knew it
with palms sweating
you played the game
waiting for your name.

Soon a summer job.
Empty.
You thought
it was your fault.

Then graduation.
Bar exam.
First job.
Empty.

So night poetry
you wrote
urging settlement
in the office.
But clients want revenge
not peace.

Now you take apart
young adversaries.
Full partner
your reward.

And they're so proud.

To Be Free

I pray the one
kept inside
so long
might be free.

To drink of life
with
long
slow
swallows.

To savor time
and
no longer
feel rushed.

To breathe deep
and full
touching
the cycles of life.

To say
Enough!
Now I will be me.

Free to work
as hard as ever.
But now working
to help
those who
hunger for hope.

For the one inside
knows that life
as it was
meant to be
is good.

But life
as it has
become
is
twisted.

And upside down.

Not Getting It

The hard
part in
dealing
with people
who don't
get it
is they
don't
get it
when you
tell them
they don't
get it.

Letting Go

You told me
all along
an adult
would be there too.

Now it's eight
twelve-year-olds
going to a
rock concert
alone with thousands
of people.

NO, YOU
CAN'T GO!
THE OTHER
PARENTS
MUST BE CRAZY.

Then it
hit me.

Sometimes even
when you're right
you have to let go.

My Prodigal

My son was lost
but now is found
used to be just
a Bible line.

Then my son hit
thirteen.

Now I hold
the ring
and robe and
fatted calf
ready.

Waiting.

Bless You, My Son

Sounds like
something
you'd find
in the Bible.

But this isn't
the Bible.
It's real life.

All of a
sudden you're
eighteen
and I struggle
for words
to say.

The simplicity
of them
blows me away.

God loves you.
I do too.

The Colt

Frisky at fifteen
he struts
and prances
straining to gallop.

Growing so fast
it hurts.
All legs
and muscles.

He eyes the
girl ponies
and bucks
to be free.

But love
keeps
the rein tight.

For now.

Sandwich

The only
thing
harder
than
being
the father
of a
fourteen
year old son
is
being the
son of an
eighty-one
year old
father.

Daddy

I never called him Dad
or Father or Pop.
Always Daddy.

But I got too old
and called him
nothing
during those teen years.

When the pain
of growing
came
he said,
Just take it
a day at a time.

And I began
to know him.
That he was
not weak
but gentle.

That I was his.
My hair.
My walk.
My duty.
My hurt.

Father and son.
A link
never spoken
nor explored.

Always there.

Flag Day 1997

The plan
was to
put it
out and
remember.

He
always
flew
the
colors.

But
it
rained.

Doing it
the
next day
felt
silly

'til I
realized
it was
Father's
Day.

Soldier

That's a
joke.
He was
no soldier.

A drug
store
clerk
forced
in '42
to fight
he stayed
after the War
to feed
his family.

Going
through
old medals
and photos
I remember.

My
father.

A
good
soldier.

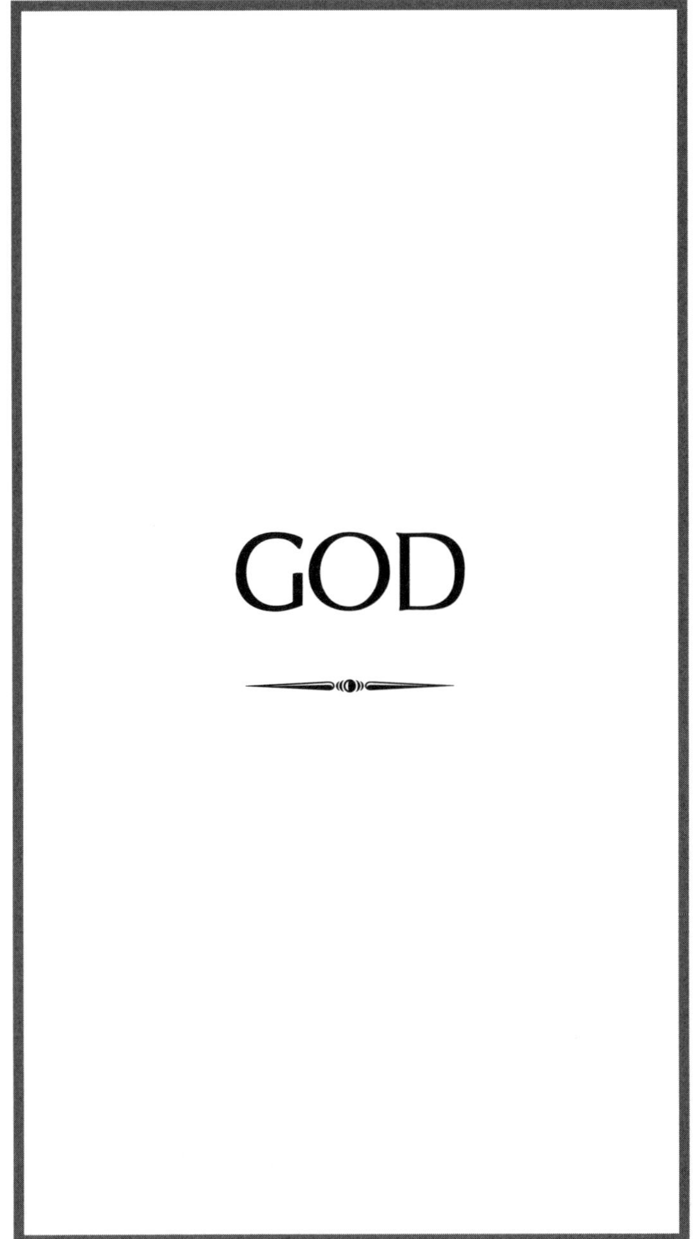

GOD

GOD

For years I was an agnostic. I left God alone and God left me alone.

Then in 1976 I met David Kidd, a fiery red-headed Presbyterian. David had followed the same path until a winter night at Brown University landed him in divinity school.

I met him a few years later and for the first time a minister made sense to me.

Then Nancy McCurley came along. A fellow church member, she entered divinity school at the age of thirty-five. Nancy is a remarkable woman of many gifts; her ministry radiates the love of God.

To them I owe these writings, bench-marks of my own faith journey.

New Year's Resolution

This past
January
I resolved
to trust
God.

Always
listening
for that
little
voice.

Mid-February
report:

Speak Up!

Councilman

Praying,
I heard
a voice.

Councilman…

It's okay,
I said.

You can
call
me Ron.

Life Insurance

And if
I should
die before
I wake
I pray
the Lord
my soul
will take.

Simple
life insurance
for a
three-year-old.

I wonder
why it
has to get
complicated.

First Glasses

The
six-year-old
sits
in the car.
Amazed.

Trees
have
leaves.

Four-eyes
to
some.

A
miracle
to
him.

Crucifix

I've never
worn one
of those
little
crosses
around
my neck.

Always been
turned off
by people
with religion
on their
sleeve.

But maybe
I'll
try one.

Keep it
under my
shirt where
nobody
can see
it.

Well
almost
nobody.

Gifts

Every
day's
a gift.

Even
the
bad
ones.

Rest

When
all
energy
is
gone
rest.

Without
guilt.

Agony

To
know
at
last
what
feeds
the
soul.

And
not
be
able
to
eat.

Earth

Fragile
beauty
hanging
in
black
backdrop
of
infinity.

One Little Light

We can
curse
the
darkness
or light
one
little
flashlight.

Always
monitoring
the batteries
and bulb.

Mercury God

God
eludes
us
like
mercury
chased
by
children's
fingers.

So
into
little
bottles
is
put.

On Your Back

God
is
not
seen
from
recliner
rockers.

But
on
your
back
in
the
desert.

Kaleidoscope

It's overwhelming.

Our need
to touch
the source
of color.

Feel
the
turning.

See
the
pattern.

But all
we get is
glimpses.

Refracted.

Temptation

And lead
us not into
temptation
but deliver
us from evil.

It's not
temptation
away from
the biggies
we need.

But those
harmless
little
things
we know
aren't
quite right.

Facets

Like a
well-cut
stone
life's
facets
shine.

Why
do we
focus
on
the one
with
the
blemish?

The Fish

Gasping
he flips
and
flops
knowing
he can
make it
back to
the
water.

He tries
again.
Again.

Again.

Exhausted
he feels
the gentle
hand scoop
him home.

Playing God

His name's
Sebastian.
Prettiest dog
I've ever seen.

And sweet.
A typical
Golden
Retriever.

When he was a
pup he wasn't
very good
in dog school.
But we got by.

Now he's sick.
The vet says it
may be cancer
but there's a choice.

Prolong it
with antibiotics
or be quick
and put him
down now.

Last Communion

For fifty
Decembers
she's been
in the
old church
kitchen.

Fixing
waffles.
Celebrating
the Season.

But this
year's
different.

She lies
in fog
knowing
they've
come to her.

Eating the
sweet
morsel
she smiles.

And leaves.

Hillsboro Presbyterian Church

Amazing mix
of people
with common faith
struggling
toward truth.

Huddling
in grief.
Celebrating joy.

Filling
sacred places
with laughter
and prayer.

Not a building
committee system
music program
holy book
or budget.

Family.

Confirmation Class

We're so proud.
Not that you
went to class
and said
the right things.

Anybody can do that.

But that you
calmly took it
for what it is.
A gift.

Not answering
all your questions
or sheltering you
from pain.

Just providing
an anchor
for life.

Black And White

The whole place moves.
Together once a year
the whole place moves.

Self-conscious
in common faith
we smile.

Rich black
preaching and song.
White theology
constantly probing.

Amazing grace.
One generation
from segregation
and we are together.

We sing.
Pray.
Eat.
Then go
to different worlds.

To have come so far
with so far to go.
Yet it's simple.

Simple
as
black and white.

Pony Prayers

The boy prays
with all his might,
God I'll be good
if you bring me a pony.

Years later
in the middle
of the night,
God I'll be good
if this sale I make.

God hears.
Sad.
The boy has not grown
though now a man.

I don't bargain
God says to himself.
For ponies or presents
or anything else.

Be good and faithful
because you are free.
To be the best
or the worst
you can possibly be.

For strength
to endure and peace
you can pray.
But not ponies.

It doesn't work
that way.

Whisper

We scream
at God
demanding
an answer.

When it
comes
in a
whisper
we can't
believe
it.

So we
keep
screaming.

Soul Light

Go
deep
inside.

Past
voices
feelings
moods.

What
do
you
find?

A light.

Barely
burning
or
glowing
golden
bright.

Restless Rumbling

It's been there
since he was twelve
or so.
A curse or blessing
who knows.

Restless rumbling
hunger for more.
Questioning.
Challenging.
Life to explore.

Never content
all becomes rut
as rumble growls
deep in his gut.

He cries,
What's wrong with me!
Why can't I just be?
What's wrong with me?

He prays for
quiet and rest
in his heart.
But the prayer
is unanswered.

The rumble won't stop.

Three a.m.

It
touches
the
soul
to
wake
and
feel
the
house.

Hearing
only
the
quiet.

Long Night

Fear
comes
not
from
dark
but
from
unknown.

Wondering
how
long
the
night
will
be.

LOVE

LOVE

It ought to be labeled *Fragile: Handle With Care.* Yet we toss it around without a thought.

Whether it's that rare bond between two souls or the easy banter only best friends share, there's just one word for it.

Go ahead, say it. Before it's too late.

Circle Of Love

You shall
love God
and love
one another
as you love
yourself.

The circle
of love.

Like children
at play
we run
around it
trying to
break in.

Not knowing
whose hands
to grasp.

Love Fear

We
overcome
fear
with
love.

But what
if what
we fear
is love?

Her Eyes

There was
a glow
about the old
man and
woman on
the crowded
pier.

Holding
hands
she gazed
out at birds
and he talked.

Sweet
I thought.
That's
us one
day.

Leaving
I walked
near them
and saw.

He was
her
eyes.

My Valentine

I remember
Valentine's Day
in eighth grade.
Too old for
shoe boxes
filled with cards
I plotted
to give
just one.

"Missing" the bus
from school
I walked home.
Couldn't help
passing her house.

Quiet I left
the red box and card
then ran
heart-pounding home.

Next morning
her smile
said she got it.
I blushed.

But no one else saw.

Light Dance

On the wall
two circles
of light
danced.

Moving
slowly
toward
each other
'til only
one shone.

Still.

The Maker and the Baker

His seventy-seven
year old hands
mix muffins.

Ready to bake!
he calls.

She comes
and spoons
them out.

A team
with golden
anniversary
passed
they spit and spat
and like it
like that.

He makes.
She bakes.

I Love You

To tell another man
you love him
is something
you just don't do.

Are you crazy?
What's the matter
with you?

But when you've been
together
in bright sun
and brooding weather
there's nothing else
to do.

Just say it.
I love you.

Soul Touching

Touching
another
soul's
rare.

Full
of
ecstasy.

And
pain.

Balloon Ride

I watch
myself
going up
in a
hot air
balloon
trusting
God will
fire the
burner.

Putting
you in
another
I wonder
if we'll
be blown
together.

Or apart.

Letting Go

Freedom
comes
after
letting
go of
those
we love
most.

JOY

JOY

In *Fire in the Belly,*[1] Sam Keen suggests a basic problem for men today is our lack of joy; we've forgotten how to relax and enjoy life.

This is a sad commentary on modern men. Unfortunately, it describes many women, teen-agers and even children, as well.

Our challenge is not simply to relax; it is to live with joy.

[1] *Fire in the Belly* by Sam Keen (Bantam Books 1991, page 171).

Hints On Living Joyfully

- Be silly once in a while.

- Laugh at yourself. And life.

- Be flexible. Change your mind.

- Give away something every day (a phone call, card, book, flower, hug).

- See the world as a place of abundance, not scarcity.

- Have your own room (or corner) and fill it with things that give you joy.

- Get in touch with nature. Look at the stars; take a deep breath of outside air; listen to the rain.

- Get excited! Stoke up that fire in your belly.

- Live every minute, even if you're just washing dishes.

- Find meaning in your work. There's got to be *something* good about it.

- Be patient with yourself. And others.

- Forgive.

- Listen to your heart.

- Pray regularly and positively, surrendering to God's will.

- Don't expect to solve the whole problem, just do what you can.

- Don't try so hard.

- Relax and feel the flow of life.

- Let the steam out.

- Do the best you can but remember: Competition breeds winners and losers. Cooperation breeds joy.

- Seek balance. Your social, physical, intellectual, spiritual and emotional selves all deserve attention.

- See life as a mystery; a process to be lived, not a problem to be solved.
- Remember your life is an unfinished story. Who can imagine what will be in the next chapter?
- Love God.
- Love others.
- Love yourself.

READINGS

A Touch of Wonder by Arthur Gordon, Jove Books (1974)

Care of the Soul by Thomas Moore, Harper Perennial (1992)

Chicken Soup for the Soul by James Canfield and Mark Hansen, Health Communications (1993)

Fire in the Belly by Sam Keen, Bantam Books (1991)

Hymns to an Unknown God by Sam Keen, Bantam Books (1994)

Iron John by Robert Bly, Addison-Wesly (1990)

King, Warrior, Magician, Lover by Robert Moore, Harper S.F. (1991)

Life's Little Instruction Book by H. Jackson Brown, Jr., Rutledge Hill Press (1991)

Peace is Every Step by Thich Nhat Hanh, Bantam Books (1991)

Running from the Law by Deborah L. Arron, Ten Speed Press (1991)

The Joyful Christian by C. S. Lewis, MacMillan (1977)

The Light in the Kitchen Window by Margaret Britton Vaughn, Bell Buckle Press (1991)

The Road Less Traveled by Scott Peck, Simon & Schuster (1978)

The Seven Habits of Highly Effective People by Stephen R. Covey, Simon & Schuster (1989)

The Tao of Leadership by John Heider, Bantam Books (1985)

Teach Only Love by Gerald G. Jampolsky, Bantam Books (1983)

To Order Copies

To order additional copies of this book please send a check or money order for $9.95 per copy to:

Radnor Press
Suite 350
2021 Richard Jones Rd.
Nashville, TN 37215

Orders of four copies or more will be processed for $7.95 per copy.